PRAISE FOR
THE THIN LINE

Mere minutes into the performance, tears were streaming down my face. The play was a reflection of my life. My struggle was there for all to see, I was not alone, and someone was putting words to what I could not. *The Thin Line* is the most accurate portrayal I have seen, heard or read. This play helped my loved ones to understand. It showed my parents a little of what was going on in my head. This play captured my emotions, my thoughts and my struggles. —*KV, recovering from anorexia*

The Thin Line is one of the most accurate examinations of the experience of eating disorders. It shows the insidious hold eating disorders develop on an otherwise rational, resourceful, reliable person; how it destroys self-confidence, judgment, and relationships; how they affect the families and friends; how they defy logic and destroy the spirit. *The Thin Line* may serve to both prevent eating disorders and to provide insight and hope to those who suffer from them. It will be a valuable tool in our attempts to defeat the "Body Wars" that plague girls and women in western culture. —*Dr. Margo Maine, author of* **The Body Wars**

The Thin Line captures the contradictory psychology of eating disorders and the frustration, fear, and confusion they evoke in others who want a simple way to make things better. The play addresses beautifully the way girls speak through their bodies, in symbolic and emotionally complicated ways, the things they cannot say or even know consciously. It will blow people away. —*Dr. Lyn Mikel Brown, author of* **Powered By Girl**

This timely program...was magnetic, relevant, and moving. It spoke directly to our audience in ways that no amount of didactic teaching could and gave our students a compelling view into the thinking process of a young woman struggling with anorexia as well as insight into the devastating effects it was having on significant others in her life. The actress...held the audience in the palm of her hand. —*Leslie Stein, Belfast Area High School, Belfast, ME*

I am writing on behalf of the Brookdale University Hospital and Medical Center to express our sincere thanks for the excellent performance...at our Grand Rounds. The performance was well received by our residents, medical students, and all in attendance. Personally, I would like to thank you...I believe the play is an extremely valuable learning tool for both professionals and lay people. —*Dr. Ira Sacker, author of* **Dying to Be Thin**, *Brooklyn, NY*

The characterization of the individuals, as well as the behaviors exhibited, were truly authentic... Following the performance, a lengthy discussion...provided an opportunity to share insights, ask questions, and point out resources. I would highly recommend *The Thin Line* to other college audiences and to anyone who is interested in learning more about eating disorders. —*Cindy Visbaras, Bates College, Lewiston, ME*

The play is powerful and speaks to everyone: both those with the condition and those who stand by feeling so helpless. I can recommend it whole-heartedly as a way to look at and begin addressing the concern of disordered eating among middle and high school girls. —*Mary Orear, Mainely Girls, Rockport, ME*

It's so real. I've been struggling with an eating disorder, and while the "real life drama" is much more intense, I am Ellen. I have Ellen's negative voice. This play really helped me see my friends' perspective. — *Anonymous*

This was one of the most powerful convo[cations] that Centre has offered in a long time. It dared to wrestle with a topic that few will even look in the face. —*Anonymous, Centre College, Danville, KY*

Your requirement that local resource people be there, identified, and included in the discussion ensures that your play serves as a catalyst for action that persists beyond the event itself. It provides an opportunity to raise the issue and discuss it in a way that strengthens the connections among those local organizations and people confronted with this challenge. —*Sharon Barker, University of Maine*

Thank you all for an excellent assembly. It was one of the most effective ones I have seen regarding eating disorders. The actress was superb and even my ninth grade advisees in the back of the auditorium were transfixed. —*Mary Sykes, Convent of the Sacred Heart, CT*

The inner negative voice enabled our post performance discussion to broaden to a wider range of adolescent issues. This program would benefit many different audiences and enlarge their understanding of the struggle a person has with an eating disorder. As one student said today, "It helps you not feel alone with it." —*Char Davidson, Choate Rosemary Hall, CT*

There has been great care taken to provide good information. The panel coming after the play is a brilliant idea! ...this was one of the best, if not the best program I've put on at Marymount. —*Kathleen de Blois, Marymount High School, Los Angeles, CA*

Thank you so much for your wonderful presentation. I think that your artful and moving portrayal(s) allowed the students to connect with the information on a much deeper, personal level. I think this kind of presentation gives permission to talk about difficult subjects and I am hopeful that the conversation will go on for a long time. —*Emily Sears Vaughn, Marlborough H.S., Los Angeles, CA*

It was an honor to present Abigail Solomon as Center of Creative Arts' St. Louis 2003 Emerging Artist...Much of the success of *The Thin Line* comes from [her] ability to connect with the audience. —*Stephanie Riven, COCA, St. Louis*

I had a girlfriend who suffered from bulimia, and it was huge for me to have seen this play, for it gave me that awareness to be very supportive of her, and to try and understand where she was coming from. If I hadn't

seen *The Thin Line* I may have dealt with it in a whole different way, which would not have been beneficial for her, or me. The basic knowledge that I attained from watching the play certainly has stuck with me, I retained it, and it has helped me in thinking about and dealing with situations that I would have no experience or knowledge about otherwise.
—*Ryan Berger, Portland, ME*

Given the response to Tuesdays night's performance here on our campus, I am sure the community has been affected positively and can build further on our mission. Without reservation, I would recommend *The Thin Line* to other college or university audiences or to any community.—*Lisa M. Sinden-Gottfried, Washington University in St. Louis, MO*

On behalf of the faculty and students at MICDS, I would like to thank you for your two passionate performances of *The Thin Line*. The play's content had a powerful and profound impact on our community and it promoted much discussion for days afterward.—*Liz Clark, Mary Institute and St. Louis Country Day School, St. Louis, MO*

The Thin Line was brought to the University for its obvious relevance to the lives of our students, many of whom struggle with eating disorders, body-image concerns, and dealing with our diet- and thinness-obsessed culture. Each presentation led to extended discussion sessions, referrals to our counseling center, conversations in classes, and a heightened awareness and sensitivity to these issues across the campus. I recall one evening in particular when I had to leave for another engagement, but a full hour after the play was over the discussion was still going strong.—*Dr. Clay Greybeal, University of New England*

OTHER BOOKS BY
ADD VERB PUBLICATIONS

Out & Allied: An Anthology of Performance Pieces Written by LGBTQ Youth & Allies, Vol. 1 (Maine Writers & Publishers Alliance Award, Best Anthology 2012)

Out & Allied: An Anthology of Performance Pieces Written by LGBTQ Youth & Allies, Vol. 2

You the Man: Add Verb's Performance and Program on Bystanders and Gender Based Violence

When Turtles Make Love: A Play on Parents and Teens and the Big Talk

Money Talks: Theatre for Financial Literacy

THE THIN LINE

A play about ending the silence on eating disorders

FIRST EDITION

Add Verb Publications

THE THIN LINE

Add Verb's Performance and Program on Coping With Eating Disorders

FIRST EDITION

© 2017, Cathy Plourde
All rights reserved

The contributors of this book may have changed names and other identifying elements of their narratives to protect privacy. *The Thin Line* is a work of fiction. The characters are a product of the playwright's imagination and any resemblance to real people is entirely coincidental. The materials in this book are for documentary purposes only and individuals and organizations are responsible for seeking their own professional guidance in any performance or educational program that would address eating disorders.

No part of this book may be used or reproduced in any manner whatsoever without written permission except in the case of brief quotations embodied in critical articles and reviews. For information contact: addverblicensing@gmail.com.

The scanning, uploading, and distribution of this book via the Internet or via any other means without the permission of the publisher is illegal and punishable by law. Please purchase only authorized editions, and do not participate or encourage piracy of copyrighted materials. Your support of the authors' rights is appreciated.

Printed in the USA
Interior and cover design by K. Larson
Cover image design by Zach Magoon

LCCNumber: 2017939476
ISBN-10: 0-9913528-5-8
ISBN-13: 978-0-9913528-5-2

Add Verb Publications

Books in Add Verb Publications catalogue may be purchased for educational, business, or sales promotional use.
For information please write: addverblicensing@gmail.com

To Ryan Fuller Bass, the student who taught me. Your work, talent, charm, and travel agent skills allowed for thousands and thousands see The Thin Line.

LICENSING INFORMATION

The Thin Line is copyright protected and all rights are reserved and are held by the author. No duplication or production without permission.

To request amateur or professional rights for performing *The Thin Line* write to: addverblicensing@gmail.com (Note that there are two Ds!)

If you are planning a reading for a group, event, or Eating Disorders Awareness Week, please send a note to the email above as we would like to be able to share how *The Thin Line* is being used around the world.

CONTENTS

Playwright's Note 12

Actors on Performing *The Thin Line* 20

The Thin Line (Annotated US Script) 24

Actor Prop/Travel Checklist 46

Site Coordinator Checklist 48

Production Guide 50

The Thin Line in Cultural Translation: Australia 69

The Thin Line (Australian Script) 73

PLAYWRIGHT'S NOTE

The Thin Line was developed out of a fair amount of research, specifically the formative work of Lyn Mikel Brown, Carol Gilligan, Amy Purcell, Sheila M. Reindl, M. Suzanne Repetto, and Catherine Steiner-Adair. New information and research continues to be made available, but the core information has remained the same. Additionally, I drew upon conversations with people who have been directly affected by eating disorders — individuals, family, friends, and medical and mental health professionals. The research and interviews together helped me to distill content and composite real experiences into invented characters.

At the first staged reading of the play, people were very moved but a friend of the teenage actor I had found to perform said, in evident frustration, "Yes, we know that our friends have this problem. What we don't know is what to *do* about it."

I took her point to heart and used this idea of "So what?" as a litmus test for most of the educational theatre that I created afterwards. An unsolicited gift from a benefactor, Bonnie Rukin, who also happened to be in that first audience, provided the funds for further research and script development workshops with actors, and I updated the script and created an educational program to accompany it. The play started touring in 2000 under the company name Add Verb Productions Arts & Education, and was performed by Jessica Peck. Curricula for middle and high schools, aligned with Maine State learning outcomes, followed a few years later. Materials to guide anyone considering producing the play are available online (www.addverbproductions.org). The play is dynamic and engaging, designed to create action and spark dialogue. But it is just a play. And as that teenager said, the audiences are most interested in what to *do* about eating disorders, which should not be lost on producers.

For me, the effort to put *The Thin Line* into the world was never about the play itself and I've not held my words precious. Instead, the focus was always about the message the script carried and maintaining respect for the audiences. The play and the program aim to leave a community stronger than it was beforehand, better equipped to address the issues, and more engaged with the local resources who will help people in the days and weeks to follow. Changes were periodically made to the script to provide solid information on questions that were frequently raised in talkbacks and to adapt to cultural and technological evolution.

The process of hiring actors was tricky and we were lucky to find a number of talented young women to travel the United States with this production. It was important to me that each one was healthy in mind and body, appeared to be of average weight, and was old enough to rent a car as touring often required a flight and then a drive! I intentionally avoided hiring actors who had eating disorders (EDs) in their past or present. I know people in recovery may be amazing activists and that the telling of their stories is a part of the personal and societal healing process; however, my primary fear was that they would be triggered by the play. I was upfront about this concern and the actors and I had long talks about their relationship to the play and its issues as a part of their preparation. Nearly always particpants in the post-performance talks, these young women grew to become passionate and knowledgeable, and audiences regularly approached them with thanks or stories of their own. The post show process is more fully addressed in the production guide, but people in recovery have been encouraged to attend performances and often speak from the audience to great effect; panel members were encouraged to maintain a professional position and not disclose their own personal history in this public context.

The biggest difference from performance to performance is in the post show discussions, which are tailored to suit the audience, whether they be school children or medical professionals. *The Thin Line has* been performed for audiences of all ages without any changes beyond the actor making subtle shifts in Ellen and Cindy to more closely align with the audience. This universality made it hard to sell sometimes, as people working in university settings did not believe that the same play being presented to middle schools students could possibly work for college-aged students, and visa versa. This is understandable, as many plays have limitations on age appropriateness; however, in the case of *The Thin Line* its fluidity is part of what makes this show special.

To further challenge the actor's job, most audiences were "captive," meaning the program was a required assembly during the school day; I'm willing to bet many were convinced before even sitting down in the auditorium or gymnasium that the play would be cheesy, condescending, and yet another case of adults telling them what to do and think. Middle school and high school audiences are especially intolerant of bad theatre, and they are not interested in being polite if they are bored or put off. Every actor knew that they had to win their audience over in the first ten seconds or it was going to be a long and uncomfortable show. It forced the actors to make the stakes high and to be true.

The script's use of direct address—speaking to the audience as if they were the actor's scene partner—helped ground the text and keep the actor honest. Speaking with truth is important because in every audience there are individuals who are struggling with eating disorders or disordered eating, and friends and family members of people who are struggling.

Working with the actor to make the most of a direct address-style performance, which is quite different from a play that has people talking with each other on the stage, is exciting and frightening: there is nowhere to hide. The connection to the audience is made even more intense as we always request that the venues have the house lights remainon *as well as* the stage lights. More often than not, the play has been done in non-theatre venues, with a negligible separation between the playing area and the audience. Sometimes the actors are faced with people scowling at them from the front row, body language revealing deep discomfort; ususally these were people currently dealing with the issue personally (which they revealed in the post-show discussion). Sometimes the audience has a pocket of people that won't stop talking; often this has been a situation of friends relating the play to a person they knew. At one school where EDs were a very present issue the actor relates that as the show progressed, one by one, the entire front row held each other's hands, many quietly weeping. The actors said that when they saw these type of things occurring mid-performance, their first instinct was to back down the intensity of their performance — especially with younger audiences — but they grew to realize that this is when they have to trust the script and stay doubly committed to the arc of the show: to back off would render the words, action, message of the play hollow. Respectfully riding the emotional energy of the audience honors the people in the room who know the truth and the devastation of EDs.

An emotional response from an audience is gratifying but a play is not a "good" play because it makes people cry. I wanted *The Thin Line* to be a moving piece of theatre, but *Primum non nocere* – "First, to do no harm." A part of the Hippocratic oath taken by medical professionals, this is a concept that is a social justice concern and does not need to compromise artistic expression or merit. This concern for safety and care was reflected in my research, and it informed what was represented in the script and what was left out. It is also one reason the play has multiple characters. As a single actor transitions in and out of the four roles, this theatrical conceit repeatedly breaks the fourth wall and reminds the audience that this is a play and not an autobiographical performance. The use of multiple related characters illustrates how eating disorders affect a whole community and are not just the experience of an individual. I also didn't want to put the main character, Ellen, in the position of being judged, becoming even more vulnerable, or further pressured to change. When someone is dealing with an eating disorder, they are busy with surviving; it is other people, the culture, attitudes, behavior, the media, the patriarchy—et cetera—who carry the responsibility of change and creating communities in which eating disorders and myriad other public and mental health challenges cannot thrive.

Of course, what a playwright, director, or producer *wants* and *intends* requires more than a wish and good intentions. As I went through the development process with *The Thin Line*, I repeatedly vetted the script with a number of types of professionals. However, the experts and I did not always agree, such as with the inclusion of Ellen's self-mutilation. A distressingly high percentage of people with an ED self-mutilate, though it is just as true that many people who self-mutilate do not have an ED; however, because it is a visible sign that may be more apt to be seen by friends rather than adults I felt it was important to find a non-glamorizing, non-alramist way to include the issue. Right after I made this change to the script, an attending panelist told me that I had made a bad choice and these students were too young to know about this issue. Sure enough, not long into the audience discussion one of the middle schoolers raised her hand and asked, "Why did the girl cut herself?" The professional did not want to answer the question and almost blew over it, saying "I don't know that we need to talk about that. How many people even know anyone who does that?"

Middle schoolers being middle schoolers, hands shot up all over the room.

The panelist took a deep breath and then proceeded to give a very good and age appropriate explanation of how this is a cry for help and if they see something like this, they should talk to a trusted adult or the school nurse as their friend may need some help.

Mission accomplished.

Testimonials from administrators and professionals helped inspire confidence in *The Thin Line* as a quality program, and more than one new booking came because a sister school had brought it in and spoke well of the experience. However, measuring the actual impact of theatre is extraordinarily difficult to achieve and most "evidence" of educational theatre's efficacy is collected by surveys immediately following performances and likely comes under the heading of "feel good" data, and does not measure changes in attitudes and behaviors. From 2000 to 2014, we had lots of audience feedback forms but no quantifiable data. In 2010-2014, with funding from the Van Otterloo Family Foundation, I worked with a team of researchers at the University of New England to design and implement an Institutional Review Board approved longitudinal study. At this writing, the study's Primary Investigator, UNE faculty member Peter Herrick, MSed., is writing up results for peer-review publication, but the raw data supports what we believed: that students increased their knowledge, were more likely to intervene on behalf of someone they knew, and that over time much of this was sustained and many had even attempted an intervention on someone's behalf. A similar study has been undertaken by Professor Ann Taket at Deakin University in Melbourne, Australia, with positive early indicators.

The types of stories of health and recovery that have come out of 15 years of performances of *The Thin Line* and its accompanying program are exciting:

> During one performance a woman who was sitting to the side quietly cried the entire show. Afterwards she told us that she was okay, but that her tears were from a new understanding of what her family and friends had been through when she was in the grip of an eating disorder.

> A board member was talking with a friend in a grocery aisle about Add Verb. A young man walking by overheard and said, "Add Verb?! Before I saw the play I didn't know a guy could have an eating disorder. I owe Add Verb this beautiful body!"

A young audience member recognized an actor on the street in New York City. The girl's mother pulled the actor aside and said the day of the performance was the day her daughter began her recovery.

After a show at a private school in Los Angeles, the students were furious, and let the school's administration and panel professionals know it. They were angry because they felt this was the conversation they needed to have when they were in middle school, and demanded to know why it had taken so long for the school leaders to address the issue.

One mother whose university-aged daughter was in recovery said that she felt the play had been pulled out of her head, presenting her exact feelings and thoughts she experienced as her daughter and their family navigated the trajectory of the illness.

A high school student approached me as we were putting the props and extra audience handouts away to say that the play captured what was happening with her father and his declining health.

A student who was a peer moderator for a performance ran backstage just moments before the actor was to go on stage to say that when she saw the play the previous year it was a wake up call for her to get help. And because of the play, she added, she also realized her sister was in trouble and she found the courage to something about it. They were both doing okay now and were closer than ever. She said, "Thank you... and have a good show."

It was feedback like this that kept us going, kept us marketing the show, and kept us writing grant funding proposals for close to two decades.

Between 1999 and 2016 *The Thin Line* toured as an Add Verb production, and its success is shared by a number of booking agents, interns, and administrators working with Add Verb, but mostly it was the actors who traveled solo around the United States into schools, communities, and conferences equipped with only their talent and a bag of props that made it work: Jessica Peck, Ryan Bass, Nikki Lopez, Diane Cooper-Gould, Abigail Rose Solomon, Megan Hart, Susan Palmer, Amanda Huotari, Paten Hughes, and Emily Dennis (in rough chronological order). In Australia, Kyrié Capri and Madeleine Whitehead have performed a cultural translation of *The Thin Line* directed by the renowned Suzanne Chaundy, produced by Prof. Ann Taket (Deakin University, Melbourne, Victoria), who led the Australian writing team, including myself, Virginia Murray, Genevieve Pepin, and Patrick Van Der Werf.

To all of these actors, booking agents, administrative and creative teams; board members, donors and foundations; students and families who convinced their schools to book the program; and, the dedicated, passionate coordinators in each community who made the production possible, wrangled panelists and administrators: thank you. With your moving, gracious, and committed support, you have shared with literally thousands upon thousands of people the critical idea that they are not alone. There is hope. Recovery is possible.

ACTORS ON PERFORMING THE THIN LINE

Over the years the actors who performed The Thin Line *had many tales to tell of what happened during performances and in the ensuing conversations. Several of them have volunteered reflections on what it was like to perform the play and what they would share with others considering a production.* ~CP

Abby: This play is the best kind of art in that it literally moves people to take action. *The Thin Line* entertains and also saves lives. I sold and performed *The Thin Line* throughout the United States for eight years. People with eating disorders sought help after seeing this show. Cathy Plourde expertly researched and shaped the play to be as educational, helpful and safe as it could be and we never performed it without a discussion panel of experts afterwards. It is a brilliant way to get groups to talk about a difficult and often secretive subject. It helps change a community, which I have experienced first hand. And from an actor's perspective, it is a meaty, fascinating show to perform.

Abigail Rose Solomon
New York City, NY

Paten: Whenever I am asked why I perform *The Thin Line*, I close my eyes and watch a dozen faces flash across the screen inside my head. Mostly women, a couple of men. A girl with a broken smile, lots of dark eye liner around her eyes, trying desperately to appear happy but Sephora doesn't sell anything to conceal the sadness in her eyes and the sullenness to her cheeks. The bartender at a restaurant where I waited tables who I accidentally interrupted stuffing chopsticks down her throat to force herself to vomit. A friend from college in a hospital bed with IVs in her veins, just bones and a thin layer of flesh.

Toward the end of the show the evil voice of the eating disorder, reflects on photographs of all of the lives she has claimed. As I picture each of these women and men, I know that *The Thin Line* saves lives.

I would urge any actress just starting out to find this show: the script gives you all of the tools to guide you through the action and your performance. It is a study in acting. In the most surprising ways, you will learn something new from each show no matter how many times you get up on the stage. Not every performance is going to be fun: maybe a fourteen year-old boy will be laughing or distracting you. What you won't know is whether this lash-out is because he's uncomfortable: perhaps he has an older sister, and perhaps she's been throwing up her food recently. Stick with each performance. They will unlock things inside of you that you didn't know were there, and they will drive the important conversation of what an eating disorder is, who we love that is suffering from one, and what we can do to help.

If you can do this show, you must. I hope it is a rich and full adventure for you, and I'm grateful for your courageous voice. Together, I hope we can make a lasting impact on this quiet disease that permeates the quality of so many lives.

Paten Lauren Hughes
New York City, NY

Jessica: My involvement in *The Thin Line* came about rather serendipitously and I have been forever grateful to the universe for connecting me with Cathy Plourde that day, late summer of 1999. I was in my mid-twenties when I was cast. Though my life was touched by a best friend from elementary school and later a college roommate both of whom struggled with an eating disorder, I didn't know how to be a supportive friend to someone with a life-threatening mental illness and as a result, lost those friendships. Performing *The Thin Line* was not only an education into the world of this secretive public health concern, it was a kind of therapy for me as well. I learned that the friend or family member of the person with the eating disorder can only be consistent with words and actions of love toward her friend and one day, when this person needs to hear the words, "I love you and I'm scared for you," those words will sink in.

The story-telling nature of this piece reaches out to the audience in a way that propels the audience into action. It is designed to resonate on some level with every individual in the audience: the one suffering with the eating disorder, the friend, the family member, and the person unaware that he or she may know someone with an eating disorder.

Being a post-show participant was difficult and rewarding. It was difficult because I felt like I didn't have the answers. What is interesting is that even the experts on the panel claimed to not have the answers either. Eating disorders, like the individuals who live with them, vary greatly among sufferers and there is no one right way to approach this illness. I found the panel to be rewarding because of the connection that the audience was able to make with the panelists after the show. The play delivers the message, but the discussion afterwards is where the healing begins.

I began my professional career as an actor and am now in the field of healthcare. I'd say *The Thin Line* was a big influence in my life and subsequent career choice.

Jessica Peck-Lindsey
Portland, ME

Ryan: Since 2000 *The Thin Line* has been a catalyst for eating disorder awareness and prevention. As both an actor and a booking agent for the program, I have witnessed the enormous difference *The Thin Line* makes as it provides language and opens up a safe space for discussion to happen around eating disorders — illnesses so often shrouded in secrecy and taboo. It is a play that both captivates and educates the audience. Whether the communities that receive the program are middle schools or universities, rural or urban, the play never fails to enthrall the audience, engage them in meaningful discussion, and leave the community with hope, empowerment, knowledge of where to go for support, and ideas for action and prevention.

Ryan Bass
Boulder, CO

ANNOTATED SCRIPT AND PRODUCTION NOTES

This is an annotated version of the US script for The Thin Line, *with acting and staging tips as well as dramatrugical information that may be useful in understanding the characters. The National Eating Disorders Association and many other advocacy organizations have excellent materials available on their websites to ground directors and actors in knowledge about EDs.*

STAGING, COSTUMES, AND PROPS

It is intended that one person play all the roles. In some cases, such as a script reading, it may be easier to have different readers for each role. Transitions or beats between characters require both a physical and vocal shift, and cue audience to the change in character.[1]

ELLEN has a table and chair center stage pre-set with art supplies: cup or pencil holder with paint brushes or colored pencils; pencil box; rubber bands; ruler; art pad; a very wide-tipped black or blue marker. Actor wears a nondescript/neutral outfit, including quiet shoes. ELLEN wears an oversize shirt (pre-set over back of her chair). The VOICE wears sunglasses, which are preset and to remain on the table when not being used. A small photo album or tablet is downstage edge of the table and out of the way. ELLEN'S MOTHER's chair is SL, pre-set with reading glasses which get placed on table for future transitions. CINDY has a chair DR, and may leave a capped bottle of water on floor next to chair.

Ideal paying area is approximately 15' wide by 12' deep. Even if available space is larger than this, confining to roughly this size facilitates transitions between characters.

---

1 Two tips for actors: First, as soon as blocking has been set, I recommend the very next rehearsal be with the script in hand and with a small audience. This will give a physical understanding of how to handle the direct address style of the play and will minimize backsliding: essentially the audience is your scene partner, albeit without lines, and you would not normally rehearse a play without your scene partner! People love to be involved in the development of the play rehearsal process and they will be very supportive. Second, there is great value in doing table work and learning the lines of one character at a time, to get the full arc of the character's journey through the play; however, include memorizing the blocking and the lines of the characters who come just before and just after at the same time in order to begin to build sense memory of the transitions. When your mind blanks, your body and location should get you out of a pinch.

THE THIN LINE
by Cathy Plourde

Copyright © CATHY PLOURDE. 2000, 2002, 2009, 2015, 2017.

DO NOT DUPLICATE OR DISTRIBUTE OR PERFORM
WITHOUT PERMISSION FROM PLAYWRIGHT
License inquiries to: addverblicensing@gmail.com

THE THIN LINE

To begin, a moderator introduces the play, including naming the writer, actor, director, running time (approximately 30 minutes), and brief note of post-performance plan. A sample script is available in the production guide materials that follow.

(CINDY enters as though she just left someone in the wings.)

1. CINDY

This lady just asked me how I was doing. I said "Oh, fine!" I should have said: "I'm not bad. I could be worse. You know, I could have an eating disorder like my friend Ellen." I'd like to see what would have happened if I had told her how I'm really doing: "Well, my best friend's been on a series of whacko diets, has been regularly throwing up for I don't know how long now, has made me promise not to tell, and basically is scaring the hell out of me. Thanks for asking, and how are you?"

She was just being polite — I know, but how many times are you asked, "How are you?" and you say "Fine!" because you're expected to say "Fine!" and then move on?[2]

Maybe it's a game and if I pretend it's fine it will be fine.

---

[2] Cindy is generally polite, but she's had it with hypocrisy and is distraught with the realization Ellen is in serious danger. It makes her a little sarcastic.

Well, no. I'm done pretending because it's not a game anymore. My best friend Ellen is dying a slow death right before our eyes. I'm not being dramatic. This is real. What do I do now? It's so hard to know what to do. Do I risk our friendship and tell? If I tell and no one does anything will I lose my friend for good? Why doesn't anybody else see she's got a problem? Why doesn't her coach see it? What about her parents? And if they *do* see what's happening and can't do anything about it, what makes me think I could help her? If I don't say anything it's like I'm agreeing with her. But I don't agree. And the longer I don't say anything the worse she gets, disappearing before our very eyes like some dumb magic trick gone wrong. I need to know what to do.[3]

2. ELLEN

(Crosses US, puts on ELLEN's shirt, and sits at the table with art supplies, drawing pad, and loose pages of drawings in front of her, one of which is a torso and head that fills the page. She shades in an area of the drawing or is doodling. She's tired of the questions. She knows people are waiting for answers. Having acknowledged the audience as her scene partner, she mocks others who have asked this question before:)

"Ellll-en, what's the matter with you?" What's my problem? I could ask what's yours. Why do I have to have a problem before anybody cares that I exist? And then I *still* don't exist because they don't see *me* they see "*someone with an eating disorder.*" It didn't happen overnight, like I crossed

---

[3] Don't rush the end of the monologues. Completely land/finish the beat before moving into the next character.

over a line or something. So what did happen? How did
I get right here, right now?[4] Is it the media's fault? News
flash: *Girl Killed By Cosmo and Vogue; Seventeen Magazine
Suspected Accomplice!* If looking at malnourished models
and actors were all it took, wouldn't everyone have an
eating disorder? ...Was I abused? Do you think I'd tell you?
...I know it happens. ...So, am I trying to get attention? Well
aren't we all? Have I got horrible parents? Or am I just
crazy? Yeah, well, this world is crazy. You've gotta walk a
thin line[5] to get by. Be smart, but not too smart; be pretty,
but not too pretty or everybody thinks you're a snob, or
everybody thinks you don't have a brain. The rules change
everyday and everything stays the same. Everybody just
assumes they know everything about you when you aren't
even sure you know yourself. After a while, that voice
inside your head is the only one that makes any sense.

3. VOICE

*(Leaving ELLEN'S oversized shirt on the chair, she
puts on sunglasses to become the VOICE. Loud and
boisterous, slick and slimy, sugary sweet and sincerely
insincere, and always charming with the threat of
violence, the VOICE has ELLEN under her control.
The VOICE sees the audience and has a sudden idea
of how to torment ELLEN. As though the audience
is in on her plan, she takes pencil holder and sneaks
DS around the table and steps into the space formerly*

---

4 Sharp and intelligent, Ellen's sarcastic approach identifies how much she already knows about eating disorders. She doesn't minimize the experience of anyone else but she is not giving away her situation. In fact everyone's situation is different and it is often a combination of issues.
5 Forget that this is the title of the play—it doesn't need over emphasis.

occupied by ELLEN to wake her. She remains standing throughout.)

Gooooooood morning! It's rise and shine, and —

(The VOICE slams the cup down so pencils spill everywhere and addresses ELLEN at eye level as if in a mirror directly in front of her. She is in ELLEN's space.[6])

— *hold it right there,* Ellen, because I'm your first waking thought. Now, what is it you are *not* going to eat today, and how will you burn off all the calories you're charged with for even thinking about food? Little Miss Perfect, Miss Do-Goody-Goody. You're about as perfect as dirt. How can you even be seen in public?

(To Audience) Oh! Who am I? Why, I'm Ms. Negativity, Ellen's personal trainer and I've taken over. *(To ELLEN, glasses are back on)* Now where were we, let's see… Ah! The gut! Yes, your flabby, ugly, fat belly. Disgusting. Now, whenever you stand up in class or meet someone new or walk down the street, ask yourself what do they think of you and your *big fat stomach*, Ellie-Belly, got that?

(The VOICE removes glasses, steps out from behind the table DS to address the audience directly. Enthusiasm and glee grow with each myth.)

Wait. The rest of you out there are wondering what right do I have, where do I get my nerve telling this girl to hate her body? What you don't understand is that her world

---

[6] To help the audience know when the Voice is talking **to** Ellen, keep the glasses on and stay focused on where Ellen would be, but remove them when addressing the audience. The sunglasses serve as a mask and hide the eyes. Caution: too much head movement when the glasses are on looks silly.

is spinning out of control, that she happens to believe that she can control this one part of her life—that she can change her body. She's not alone. There's a Western world out there just dying to be thin, stuck in a web of myths and misconceptions!

Myth number one is that an eating disorder is a "rich white girl syndrome." Actually, more and more boys are falling prey, and I could care less how much money you and your family's got or what color your skin is.[7] Second is the beauty myth! The media feeds the national obsession with celebrities and dictates standards of beauty—never mind that it took a team of eight and computer generated body parts to get the perfect photo of that cover girl.[8] Third?! We have scientists and medical specialists who make the girl out to be a pathological freak, while really, what what's happening is only a *symptom* of what's wrong: wrong with her, wrong with you, and wrong with the world.[9]

And finally, the biggest misconception of all is that the problem is *Ellen*! And since no one is willing to talk about it, well, that just makes it all the easier for me, the ever more powerful internal voice deep inside Ellen's head.

> (*She reloads her sunglasses, and steps between ELLEN's chair and the table. Returning back to ELLEN in the mirror, back to business, a promise and a threat.*)

---

[7] At this writing, minorities and males were in the fastest growing groups of people affected by EDs. Adult on-set of EDs is increasingly common.

[8] Maybe someday this will be illegal. Negative effects of media and image manipulation are well documented.

[9] Everyone who has a serious illness or trauma wants to be allowed to live as a whole complex person, and not have one's identity singly defined and over-simplified by a label As Mom says later, it is a part of Ellen, yet not all of her..

Yes, Ellen. Me and my negativity loops in continuous play in your head, building on your worst nightmares, your secret fears. The medical term "anorexia" *(she has written the word out on the drawing pad[10], and rips it out to hold for the audience to read)* means "absence of hunger or appetite" but you and I alone know that that's not true, that you have a huge appetite. You're extremely hungry. But you're willing to deny yourself your existence. *(Lets page float to the ground SR next to the table.)* They say "bulimia" *(again, writes the word, rips it out, and holds it to be read)* is an "oxen hunger." "An uncontrolled consumption!" But that's not true either, because you and me kid, we *can* control it, and if need be, we can make sure that what goes in *will* come out.

> *(Crumples the sheet into a wad, tosses on the floor with the other mess, and then peeks at audience over sunglasses.)*

And those people out there are going to sit and watch you swallow yourself whole.

4. ELLEN

> *(Returns sunglasses to DR corner of the table, steps out, and puts on the oversized shirt. ELLEN turns to see the mess on the floor, and then sees the audience seeing her seeing it, too. She quickly picks everything up, and during the following speech everything gets put away — papers smoothed and clipped in the drawing pad, pens and marker put into the pencil box and secured with a rubber band. The drawing of the figure*

---

10 Until the spelling and spacing of anorexia and bulimia becomes muscle memory, writing the word lightly in pencil, invisible to the audience for the marker to trace on respective pages makes this go smoothly.

is left accessible for later. She speaks to distract us from her tidying and embarrasment.)

Well, the first time I went on a diet and really started exercising was when I was ten. Maybe nine.[11] It was the summer I spent with my friend Cindy's family on the Cape. Cindy and I would exercise with her older sister every morning and then spend the day at the beach. We lived in our bathing suits the whole time. Well, Cindy lived in her bathing suit; *I* lived in my bathing suit and an over-sized T-shirt. That's when things started to change. You know, with my body. Suddenly, everything's about make-up and clothes and friends and who's got a boyfriend and whether or not you've had sex yet. When I was little, my father's annoying nickname for me was Ellie-Belly.[12] Well, I got home from that vacation and my father said "Ellie! No more belly! Now what do I call you?"[13] *(Furious) How about using my name, Dad?* But he was right. My belly was gone. And that felt good.

You know, everyone does it. Even the girls who aren't really on diets pretend to be because everyone else is doing it. And if my friend is thinner than me and she's on a diet, well, maybe that means I'm fat, maybe that means I should

---

11 Ellen is progressively more ill with each monologue, which she can play as trying to be strong (rather than telegraphing weak or sick). Here, finally, she's willing to share some of what her journey has been like, but by the end of monologue ,#4 the Voice takes over and gets the best of her.
12 While it is more recognized that bullying and abusive language are detrimental, it is hard to believe that a term intended as endearment can have such a devastating effect on some people. But it can.
13 Unfortunately many adults feel awkward when children's bodies, especially girls, start changing. Culturally accepted objectification of women has become a public health issue, especially for those who are susceptible to EDs and other risks. His observation of her weightloss evokes anger from Ellen and there's lots more where that came from.

be on a diet, too. It's like being in a club. Or getting the same kind of clothes as everyone else. It's what you *have* to do. *(She is good at this.)* It's a game, a contest to see who's the best expert on rice cakes, fat-grams, laxatives, how to fool your parents into thinking you've eaten. And how many times to run up and down the stairs to burn off one piece of chocolate.[14]

> *(Takes off the over-shirt for this last line, leaves it crumpled on the table, and strides DSL as if to the stairs for a run. She stops at the MOTHER's chair with back to the audience to compose physically and put on the glasses for the transformation.)*

5. THE MOTHER

> *(Turning to take in the audience, and then to regard her daughter's room and art table, the MOTHER gradually approaches the table as she talks, finding a moment in the speech to neaten the crumpled shirt.)*

She was the perfect baby. No fussing, ever. She was always happy. Now she only looks happy when she's sleeping or doing her artwork. She's such a perfectionist.[15] I thought at first that what Ellen was going through was just Ellen pulling away, growing up, trying to be her own person... I thought the best thing to do was just let her be. To back off.

---

14 When people feel entitled to comment on other people's bodies, it can have an unintended effect; we tend to praise people who have lost weight, in turn reinforcing self-loathing of body, and feeding an unhealthy spiral. It's also amazing to consider how ED behaviors are a silent scream for help, and yet, bystanders have few skills and great trepidation of "butting in."

15 The apple may not have fallen far from the tree. One of the barriers to youth getting help is that the adults in their lives have their own, perhaps unresolved, issues.

I had no idea.[16]

It's hard to believe that the Ellen who created this—

(Indicating the same drawing ELLEN had been working on.)

—is the same Ellen who transforms into a monster. Crying, screaming, swearing, throwing, punching, scratching. Like a caged animal. Like we are the enemy. We had a fight last night, and finally, we just held her. Her father and I stood there with her in between us and we held her until we could feel the rage wash out of her body, leaving her limp, hardly conscious. We put her to bed, like we did when she was a baby, and we got her into her pajamas. It's awful to see how little there is to her body. And worse. How could it be worse? Her arms and her stomach were covered with thin lines, some hardly perceptible, others quite fresh with scabs. It took me a few moments before I realized that Ellen has been *cutting* herself. More torture. More pain.

(She confronts the audience, turning her shame to defensiveness to hide her fear.)

You look at me and you ask yourself could it be my fault, her mother's fault? Or did her father push her too hard?[17] Did we put her on a diet? Did we teach her that in order to be worth anything what matters are her looks, her body, instead of her mind and her love? *I don't know.* Don't you

---

16 The Mother believes this is the worst of the crisis. However, this is only the beginning and she has no idea how bad it will get over the next months. The shame of having people know her daughter is ill is still important to her. Her emotional journey is made more complex over the arc of the play. Let her breath find the ebb and flow of the circumstances..
17 Trying here to not throw mothers under the bus, and to include fathers as culpable.

think if there were something simple to be done to fix it all, her father and I would have tried it already? If you content yourself with blaming us then none of us have to stop and figure out how we can fix this.

> *(Pivots and leaves glasses DL on the table and swaps them for the sunglasses before whirling around in barely controlled fury to address the audience as the VOICE.)*

6. THE VOICE

Fix it? Fix it? Like a broken shoe or television? Ha! Give me time, and I'll take the parents out, too.[18]

> *(She flips the MOTHER's chair over and inhabits ELLEN's space, again speaking to ELLEN as though she's directly in front of her, eye to eye.)*

They say they love you, but Ellen, your parents are going to look at you one day real soon, at you, their *precious* daughter, and they'll let you know that they hate you. You'll see it in your father's eyes and you'll hear it in your mother's voice, and then, yes, the next time I tell you something...

> *(She happens upon the figure drawing, coldly rips it, and tosses it aside.)*

...you'll listen.

---

18 We get to see what violence the Voice is capable of, representing the deep anger inside Ellen. The more Ellen's secret is out, the harder the Voice has to work to deceive everyone and still control Ellen. Often people who have had eating disorders have said that the Voice is actually much worse than what's here, but we can't abuse an audience — we need them to come along with us and not shut down.

(Crosses DSC, removing glasses to speak to the audience, cold and clinical.)

You're fed the *thin* line early on. Somehow those messages everybody gets growing up—be *nice*, be *good*, be *responsible*, avoid conflict, put others before yourself, don't hurt other people's feelings even if it means ignoring your own—somehow those messages become monsters. Bubble Butt. Fat Cow. Wide Load. Hey, Tubba! *(Sing-song.)* Fatty-fatty two-by-four/Can't fit through the kitchen door. Innocent name-calling? *Sticks and stones can break my bones*, but names...names will scar you for life. *(She notices that ELLEN needs to be put back into line.)* Oh—excuse me—I can't leave her alone for a moment.

(She is back at ELLEN's chair. She puts on the shirt and takes over, aggressively, to ELLEN.)

What did your neighbor just say to you? "Ellen, you look healthy *today?*" You know what that means, what *healthy* means. That means you look fat, fat like her. That's what she's trying to do to you, make you fat like her. Drop and give me twenty. Now, Ellie.

(Crosses DS of the table, now as ELLEN, gets on floor to do crunches, fast and furious, her count to reach twenty becomes progressively more difficult.[19] The audience may not hear every number, but they are counting with her. Done, she is dazed. She realizes the audience has seen her behavior. She struggles to her feet, leaves the sunglasses on the table. Her vulnerability and strength of will are both visible. Deep shame and anger fight it out in the next monologue, building

---

19 Exercise as self-punishment. The physiology of her body is beginning to fail her, and yet the body's will to live is incredible. Problems with blood pressure and circulation make her lightheaded when she gets up.

> *to her breaking point. Eye contact with audience is more difficult. She clutches herself in her oversized shirt.)*

7. ELLEN

I know how hideous I look. I'm dying to be heard, to find someone who understands. *I'm trying.* This is not fun for me. People think it's a big joke. They talk behind my back. Or they talk to me like I'm an infant who can't understand anything, or like I'm going to fall apart any second. It'd be nice to not be treated like I was a walking contagious disease[20] by people who *used* to be my friends. There used to be more to know about me than how many ounces I've gained or lost today, but that's all my mother and father and doctors care about. It's not that I don't want to grow up, it just that things get harder and harder to control, and you get more and more responsibility at the same time. I've got all the responsibility I can handle now. I don't want any more!

> *(She sweeps everything off the table with fury, leaving her exhausted and barely able to hold it together.)*

They tell me I'm at a crossroads. My blood pressure can't go any lower or I will die. They ask me why I don't want to live. Of course I want to live. Why don't they ask me questions I can answer? I am so ashamed.

---

20 A heartbreaking moment from one post show question: "Are eating disorders contagious?" You could call it a social contagion, and EDs seems to cluster. One unhappy, hurting person can exert a lot of control over and damage on a peer group.

(Leaves the shirt on the table in exchange for the MOTHER'S glasses. She takes DSC and is still.)

8. THE MOTHER

I'm almost ashamed to admit it, but we were scared. It was a relief when Ellen started eating again. We pulled through as a family and we thought the worst was over. A commitment to what was important. It was hard sometimes but also nice. Healthful foods, mealtimes together. Help from therapists, dieticians, doctors — wonderful professionals who told us so much we needed to know. But it was the *ants* that told us the truth.[21] Ants marching in and out of the storage room closet, the junk room. We were busy, so we called the professionals. The exterminator asked us why we stored so much snack food in the closet, and told us we might want to use zip-up baggies or plastic storage containers instead of shoe boxes for food and that would prevent ants from being attracted to our junk room. Do you understand? That's how we found out about Ellen's binging, hording food, and binging. We had thought she was better. Now, the drains haven't been working right and this week we got home to find the basement flooded, a pipe burst, and, *again*, we called the professionals. The plumbers suggested that we either install a garbage disposal, or stop putting excessive amounts of food down the drain. The way they said it they *knew*. They were just being polite. Apparently they had seen this before. They

---

21 It's an oversimplification, but an eating disorder can morph, maybe from anorexia to bulimia, or other addictive or self-harming behaviors may be employed as the illness is "threatened" with recovery.

didn't want to say to me and my husband that *"The reason the pipes have burst is because your daughter has thrown up so much food that the pipes couldn't handle it."*[22] We had thought she was getting better. We thought we were handling it. We thought things were working out.

> *(Turns back for transition, glasses left on the table, crosses to sit in the DR chair as if in a waiting room at a hospital. CINDY is agitated.)*

9. CINDY

Ellen and I would always work out together and then when it was clear that she had a problem it made me not want to go with her anymore. I continued to go to the gym with her because I felt as though I should keep an eye on her, you know, in case something happened. I felt responsible, and I felt like I should help her. But I wasn't helping. I was making *myself* sick—sick with worry. And I have my own problems to deal with. *I* don't starve myself and then eat the contents of a refrigerator to solve *my* problems.

> *(She feels badly for saying this.)*

I really thought about giving up—

> *(Stands to speak to ELLEN at fixed point.[23])*

Fine. If you want to kill yourself trying to be thin, well fine, if that's what makes you happy.

---

22   This happens. Acid from stomach fluids wreaks havoc on metal pipes.
23   Place Ellen forward or off center but not to wings.

(To audience. She may sit during this speech but will get back up to speak to ELLEN.)

Except Ellen is not happy. And neither am I. I talked to a couple friends but they weren't exactly helpful. Everybody seems to know someone who's got a problem and no one knows what to do. And there's a group of people around here who have nothing better to do than make fun of other people. The best advice I got was from my brother Brian, of all people, and he said his friend Calvin got all intense about food because he had to keep his weight exact for wrestling. It got so bad that he passed out in the sauna trying to lose weight before anyone figured out there was a problem, and he wound up in the hospital for weeks. Calvin's well enough to come to classes again, but he's not going back to wrestling anytime soon. Something about his heart and electrolytes—it's that serious. My brother said if I was really that worried about Ellen I should talk to the counselor who's working with Calvin.[24] And based on what's happened I'm glad I did. No matter how much I want to help her to get better—I can't get better for her. She has to do it. And I have to be honest with her. I have to be honest with her until she can learn to be honest with herself. So, I finally talked to Ellen.

(To ELLEN, and then back to audience)

I can't go to the gym with you anymore, because I'm scared, because I feel like I'm helping you abuse yourself. Get some help, I told her, *and I'll go with you if you want.* She was pissed. No, I mean *really* angry. And she said things that no friend

---

[24] Boys and men can get EDs. They also have power in helping/hurting people's recovery due to sexist social norms.

would ever say. Then she informed me that she didn't need help because she was in control.[25]

(Returns to chair, seated or standing behind it.)

Ellen was admitted to the hospital a few days ago, and they don't know how long she'll have to be here. I'm trying not to think about it, trying not to think that maybe if I had said something sooner...maybe if I had tried to...if I could have...*No*. I can't think like that. It wasn't my fault. For the first time in months, I was telling her the truth.

(Finishes beat, returns to table to transition into the VOICE with sunglasses. Lounges thoughtfully before addressing audience.)

10. VOICE

To be honest, I couldn't tell you how or why my negativity and I can make some people develop an eating disorder and yet leave others unaffected. Everyone's different. I try to get them young, but any age is fine with me. By the time they realize they're *not* in control, well...

(This makes the VOICE happy. Glasses back on before turning to table to exchange sunglasses for the shirt again, this time draped over shoulders like a blanket. Faces audience and steps DSC away from the table, alone and vulnerable, ELLEN is very ill and is trying hard to not break down.[26])

---

25 Recognize how devastating and difficult relationships with friends can be. It took courage to confront Ellen, and whatever Ellen responded with was hurtful and harsh.
26 Stepping down and away from table presents a strong sense of Ellen's vulnerability and weakness. It also makes it easier to drop the shirt DS far enough to give the Mother some acting room.

11. ELLEN

At first... I felt powerful. Strong. And now...I can hardly...

It's not about eating. But it's the one thing I can control. My life is out of control, and no one will leave me alone. I'm sick of this. And so afraid. I know I am walking a thin line. I'm so disgusting. You don't know. *(Whispers through the tears.)* I don't think I can do this.

> *(She pivots her back to the audience and lets the shirt drop to the floor. Steps to retrieve sunglasses and tablet or photo album, faces front as the VOICE, flipping through the pictures.)*

12. VOICE

Mmh — some of my best work. This woman here: a $200 dollar a day food habit. She went shopping on the way home from work, buying exactly the same things she bought the day before, didn't wait to get home to start eating, didn't stop until she ate everything, threw it up, and then off to bed.[27] Next day, she'd do the same thing all over again. Kidney failure.[28]

Now this one — she should have won an Oscar! Academy Award material! No one had *any idea* she had an eating disorder.[29] And look at this guy here — here, a size 64 waist pants, here, a size 32. Same person. The epitaph should have read, "Here lies the body of a yo-yo dieter, who lost and

---

27 Ritualized eating and purging is not uncommon.
28 Bulimia doesn't kill you, exactly; rather, the body's organs shut down.
29 A comment on Hollywood and on the deep secrecy characteristic of EDs.

gained the same 100 pounds 10 times over." Heart failure. Oh—and this girl. I was in and out in nine months.[30] Mission accomplished.

You show me any family photo album, and I'll tell you something you don't want to know.[31]

> *(Spins returning glasses and photos, exchanged for glasses. The MOTHER turns front considers the audience and also ELLEN's shirt on the floor before picking it up during the monologue.)*

13. THE MOTHER

I don't know what will happen. That's the hardest part. Some days are better than others. I hated the eating disorder. It sounds selfish, but I resented it interfering with how I want to live my life. It's a parasite bent on destroying its host. It crept into my daughter's mind, into our house and into our lives, and I wanted it to go—*leave us alone, give us back our family.*[32] But that's not how it works. The eating disorder isn't Ellen, but is a *part* of Ellen, and it's hard, but it needs just as much love as the rest of her. I need to love all of Ellen.

> *(Turns to leaves glasses, crosses SR to Cindy's chair.)*

---

30 With young bodies, the effects of EDs can be quick and deadly.
31 Secrets fuel EDs. Every family has secrets and shame which manifest difficulties.
32 This speech points to how important it is for the people surrounding someone who is ill to get their own support. Mom clearly has done so, and can be honest and not frozen with shame. Also, this is the third time Mom talks about bugs.

14. CINDY

They finally let me see her.

(DS, as if stepping into ELLEN's hospital room. The shock of seeing the small body attached to medical equipment passes over CINDY's face.)

I said, "Ellen, we're friends. No matter what you say or do, it will not change that we are friends." When I told her that, for that moment, I had her, like I had gotten through just a little bit.[33] She seems intent on testing me, and twisting what I say, just to see if I mean it, to see what's real. But at least now I'm not carrying her secret anymore. There are people who know what's going on, and together we hope... we hope we can make it.[34] Ellen may think she's alone, she may tell me to leave her alone, but she's not alone. And neither am I. Thank you.

---

33 After one show, a woman identified herself as being in recovery and indicated to the woman sitting next to her. She said that this was the friend who had kept saying, "I love you" and "You are enough" and one day she finally heard it; she told the actor and audience that that was the beginning of her recovery.

34 We need to land the play on a note of hope. Recovery is not guaranteed but it is possible.

ACTOR PROP/TRAVEL CHECKLIST

You will find a routine if you tour the show with any frequency but it's still helpful to keep a checklist if you don't have a stage manager, and to double check before things get started.

PROPS

___ Costume

___ Oversided shirt

___ Pencil box with pencils, brushes, rubber bands, clips

___ Marker and Drawing pad

___ Artwork for ripping

___ Cup for pencils

___ Voice's sunglasses

___ Voice's Photo album or tablet

___ Mom's glasses on Mom's chair

___ Water bottle by Cindy's chair (no-spill or sport top)

OTHER

___ Regular and emergency contact information for site coordinator

___ All travel documents (ID, directions, confirmation numbers, etc.)

___ Copies of Moderator and Panel materials (often needed!)

ON-SITE

___ Sound check

___ Light check

___ Furniture: table, three chairs, and clear acting space

___ Re-set props after run-thru or warm-up

___ Moderator check-in; identify stage entrance and exit, coordinate when to begin and how you will end show

___ Meet the panel, confirm panelist chairs and mic ready

COSTUMING SUGGESTIONS

- Keep it neutral, not too trendy, and plausible for the age range of characters.
- If wearing V-necks tops, be mindful of "the view" audience has when you lean over — if it is too low, it can be an issue with immature audiences and you will be upstaged by your girls. Sorry.
- Pants and top that accomodate a clip-on mic and will work for the sit-ups.
- The over-shirt needs to be easy to slide on and off, so on the big side and of a fabric that is not too clingy.
- Shoes or boots easy to move in and not noisy.

SITE COORDINATOR CHECKLIST

This list should be given to the person responsible for producing the play at a location.

___ Confirm date with health professionals, coaches, or others influential with your community as regards the issue.

___ Double check performance and scheduling conflicts: bells, intercom interference, sporting events, school events?

___ Provide actor with travel arrangements (if applicable):
   1. Flight reservations
   2. Airport pickup/return
   3. Lodging arrangements
   4. Transportation to performance site

___ Provide actor with your preferred as well as emergency contact information (this is important!).

___ Provide actor with information about the venue, size of audience, panel, and other arrangements.

___ Secure a moderator, panel members, and health professionals for post-show debriefing. Clarify that this is not the time or place to disclose any personal diagnosis or recovery.

___ Plan post-show debriefing/talk-back, and facilitators for small group discussions if needed.

___ Supply moderator panel members facilitators with **The Role of the Moderator, Moderator Script, Tips for the Moderator and Panelists,** and *The Thin Line* **Plot Summary** in advance of the performance day.

___ Secure room and resources to be available for crisis intervention counseling during program.

___ If at a school, train faculty and staff in advance. Secure adults to be in "trouble zones" during performance.

___ Secure an audience! Coordinate with groups, community leaders, agencies. Colleges coiuld work with groups on campus, such as sororities and athletics, programs with psycholgy and health professions.

___ Prepare a playbill (printed program) to hand out to audience members, to include both information about the play and your local panelists/resources, and thanks to any sponsors.

___ Arrange for clip-on microphone, if needed, and tech support for the day.

___ Arrange for needed set pieces to be on stage:
  1. Three armless chairs
  2. One 4'-6' table
  3. On a 15' x 20' performing space

___ Arrange for lighting and sound technicians to meet with actor at least 30 minutes before program begins.

___ Confirm that Moderator and any facilitators have all necessary information.

___ Ready payment to be given to actor day of performance, if there is cost involved. Similarly, provide panelists or their organizations with an honorarium for their time.

PRODUCTION GUIDE

Thank you for choosing to bring *The Thin Line* to your community. Add Verb Productions is passionate about promoting understanding about eating disorders, and hopes you will find *The Thin Line* helpful in your communities' support for those who are coping with this difficult mental illness. The Production Guide covers the four basic steps to producing this play in your community:

STEP 1. PRODUCTION TEAM

STEP 2. PREPARATION

- Preparing Leadership
- Preparing Faculty and Staff
- Preparing Students

STEP 3. PROMOTION

- Promoting the Program to a Wider Community

STEP 4. PERFORMANCE & POST SHOW

- The Role of the Moderator
- Moderator and Site Coordinator Pre-Show Concerns
- Moderator Script
- Organizing a Panel
- Tips for Moderator and Panelists
- *The Thin Line* Plot Summary
- Discussion Format Options
- Sample Discussion Approach
- In the Days After *The Thin Line*

STEP 1. PRODUCTION TEAM

It's a fair assumption that if you are planning a production of *The Thin Line*, you are doing so because you wish to address an issue that is alive in your community. Producing theatre for community engagement on social issues has a different agenda from entertainment, and is rarely something that is ticketed. There are a number of things to keep in mind as you build the team that will help make this a successful event.

- Identify a dedicated site coordinator who can oversee the whole process, including logistics, outreach, and delegating.
- Find a moderator for the performance.
- Secure professional panel members to participate in a post-show discussion.
- While the actor may be active in the process, it's advised that they find a wider circle to share in the logistics in planning a performance in a community.

Be sure to have both a Site Coordinator and a Moderator. Two heads make the whole process run much more smoothly, which is of great help to the actor as well as the audience.

A helpful checklist for the site coordinator is located on pages 48 and 49.

STEP 2. PREPARATION

The make up of your intended audience will inform how much and what kind of preparation is required, and this will be different for every community. Please take into account what is the best timing for your community to participate in this program. For example, it is not advisable to present the program during testing or exam weeks, special events or spirit weeks, Fridays, or the day before school vacation. If the community is stressed by a current event such as a death or other trauma, consider rescheduling.

What follows reflects years of experience presenting *The Thin Line* in educational settings, and the basic tenants can be applied as appropriate.

PREPARING LEADERSHIP

It's critical that the administration and leadership in your community understand eating disorders can be a matter of life and death. You may need to provide reassurances that will help an administrator be confident in approving a performance of *The Thin Line*. Add Verb has taken great care in the content, pedagogy, and ethics of educating audiences on this issue. It may help to signal community readiness by detail what process you plan to use, including some of the materials that follow, and the panelists you hope to include.

PREPARING FACULTY AND STAFF

- Faculty and staff will benefit from pre-event consideration.
- Share handouts such as those by the National Eating Disorders Association available on their website.
- Model talking about eating disorders in a non-judgmental way.
- Highlight the fact that eating disorders affect everyone in the community, of all genders, ages, and demographics.
- Coordinate with any curriculum or programming (e.g., orientation, health and wellness, sports, psychology...).

It is not unusual for those who have an eating disorders to also have co-occurring or co-morbid issues, such as abuse, depression, addiction.

PREPARING STUDENTS

The Thin Line is meant to prompt serious discussion and action toward change while being sensitive to individuals in the room who may be in the danger zone or may have friends or family members dealing with an eating disorder or disordered eating. If you choose, curricula for both Middle and High School students is available at www.addverbproductions.org.

- Respectfully inform students about the presentation in advance of the production date, and give students some basic information about eating disorders.
- Inform students that people of all genders suffer from eating disorders and that the disease shows no age, socio-economic, or racial barriers. Explain that it is extremely difficult to help and support people who have an eating disorder and that this program will offer suggestions and resources to help.
- Underscore the seriousness of the disease. People in general do not understand how prevalent eating disorders and disordered eating are because those who are ill often hide their pain.
- For younger or immature audiences, explain that jokes, laughing or teasing about the issue during and after the show are completely inappropriate and could have a serious impact on someone who is struggling with an eating disorder.
- Alert students that there will be supportive professionals at the performance.

If a student requests permission to not attend, honor that request but inquire further, and without coersion, inviter parent or therapist to join the student as the program may be a good means of communication.

STEP 3. PROMOTION

There are many in your community who might benefit from attending the performance. The Add Verb Productions website <www.addverbproductions.org> has posters, press releases, video links, and promotional materials ready for you to communicate with:

- Parents/caregivers
- PTAs, School Board, Booster Clubs
- Area therapists, nutritionists, and other health professionals
- Coaches, youth-leadership advisors, or mentors
- Area nurses, counselors or administrators from other schools
- Trusted journalist

Therapists or program directors that work with eating disorders have often accompanied their clients or patients to a production and found it a helpful process.

- Send photos with press releases, as those are more likely to be printed. Avoid shock photos.
- Link to good information in any social media campaign.
- Ask area hospitals, health centers, counselors to sponsor or to co-promote.
- Offer CEUs to professionals.

STEP 4. PERFORMANCE & POST SHOW

This section of the Production Guide for *The Thin Line* addresses the role of a Moderator, assembling a panel, and preparing for the post-show discussion. Add Verb requests that each performance be followed by a minimum 30-minute talkback period that includes local professional resources. *The Thin Line* will raise awareness, concern and dialogue, but it cannot provide answers or offer treatment and medical or emotional support.

THE ROLE OF THE MODERATOR
[Site Coordinator: Please share this with your moderator in advance; also have available for day of the program.]

The Moderator greatly impacts the success of your event. Choose someone who has the respect of the community and who will be comfortable facilitating a discussion between the audience and the panel members. Having someone whose only duty is to moderator the post-show significantly helps things flow more smoothly, and allows the Site Coordinator to be supportive during the post-show discussion in other critical ways.

MODERATOR AND SITE COORDIANTOR PRE-SHOW CONCERNS

___ Adequate seating, microphones and water for the panelists?

___ Are the items above clear of the actor's playing space but easily accessible for a quick transition?

___ Are appropriate people positioned to observe the doors? If an audience member leaves, assess whether that individual is in need of support.

___ For large groups or assemblies, are traditional "trouble" spots (e.g., back and corners of the room) supervised by adults? Disturbances are distracting to the actor, and can be distressing to audience members who are taking the presentation seriously.

___ Prior to introducing the program, is the actor ready and made aware when you are about to introduce the play? She will need to be able to hear the introduction to know when she is to begin.

___ Communicate with the actor regarding the end of the show and how the transition to post-show will be managed.

Presenting on this sensitive issue signals to the community that you are willing and open to addressing other sensitive or difficult topics.

MODERATOR SCRIPT

INTRODUCING THE THIN LINE

Please turn off cell phones, alarms, and pagers at this time. *[Demonstrate with your own device.]*

Today's presentation is of *The Thin Line*.

As noted in your program, this play is performed by one actor playing multiple roles: a friend, a girl, her internal negative voice and a mother.

We've brought this play to you today in an effort to break the silence and secrecy that often surround eating disorders, which the a mental illness with the highest fatality rate in this country.

We hope this program will help you to help friends or family members who might be struggling.

The play is 30 minutes long and will be immediately followed by discussion. During this time students will be able to ask questions of professionals who are on the panel.

[Detail in brief what this will look like.]

[For younger audiences or those not used to attending a live performance:]

Please give respect not only to the actor who is concentrating, but to other the people in the room who may have friends or family who are dealing with this issue, please, no talking or joking.

[Continue:]

Thank you for your attention today, and now let's begin: *The Thin Line*, written by Cathy Plourde, directed by _____, and performed for you today by _____.

INTRODUCING POST-PERFORMANCE DISCUSSION

Thank you for being so attentive. We will begin the post-show discussion as soon as the panel has assembled. Please use this time to consider your response to the play and what you'd like the panel to talk about.

[Brief transition. Once the panelists are in place:]

Thank you to both the audience and our guest panel for being a part of our conversation today. We intend to end this part of the program at _____.

[To the panel.]

Would you each briefly introduce yourself.? Please start off by telling us your name and share something about the performance that struck a note with you.

Thank you for sharing and I'm sure we will learn a lot from you today! _____ , please let us know when we have five minutes left so we can take a final question and have final thoughts from the panel and audience.

[Follow your established protocol for the post-show discussion, encouraging audience questions. Be sure to note any distinguished guests who are in the audience who may also have valuable contributions to the conversation. Honor the time allotted for the post-show discussion.]

The site coordinator and designees can help keep the program moving, be alert to audio quality or the need to have a question repeated, pass mics around for the audience, and/or vet and organize written questions. Most importantly, keep the moderator from running over time.

ORGANIZING A PANEL

Please remember it is contractual in licensing that you do not include a panel member who will present or disclosee as having an eating disorder or being in recovery.

Selecting the panel is the most important and most difficult aspect of producing *The Thin Line*. Local resources from your community are often willing to be present as a supportive audience member, as a panel member, or a small-group leader.

Many times panelists from your local professional community are willing to volunteer their time as a charitable donation, especially as this kind of outreach can serve to build referrals. Conversely, they may require a fee for their time. Either way it is good to clear up expectations at the top.

Often, the hospital or professional practices with which your panelists are affiliated would be pleased to be asked to make a financial contribution to the play in return for credit as a sponsor.

More experts is not better on a panel, and a large panel only serves to give the community/audience less of a chance to talk. A work-around for feeling the need to have more people involved representing different kinds of expertise could be to ask them to be in attendance but seated in the audience, and for the Moderator to draw on their support as appropriate.

The rational for not having a panelist who may present or disclose experience with their own illness is for safety and to avoid unintentionally glamorizing or minimizing how life-threatening eating disorders can be.

In most cases the actor can join your panel, only as an addition and not a replacement for local resources. Although she trained as an actor and not a mental health specialist, she may be useful or informative to your discussion. The audience has developed a bond with her and may feel more comfortable in asking her a question. She can share about her process in presenting the play and responses of audiences at other performances, and pass on any question better handled by an expert.

Suggestions for possible panelists, with 2 to 3 participants (excluding the actor) being optimum:

- School nurse or guidance counselor
- LSCW, therapist, nurse or doctor who specializes in eating disorders
- Dietician or nutritionist
- Coach or fitness person educated and sensitive to the issue

Note that it's possible one of these may be the ideal moderator.

Provide panel members with the **Tips For the Moderator and Panelists** and *The Thin Line* **Plot Summary** prior to their arrival, and brief them on the post-show discussion strategy.

Some the most moving moments in a post-show occur near the end when, after the audience has had time to ask questions and hear about local resources. It is not unusual for a person or their family member who has gotten help to find the courage to share their response to the play and how eating disorders have affected them personally.

TIPS FOR MODERATOR AND PANELISTS

[Site Coordinator: Please distribute copies of this for your moderator and panelists in advance; also have available for day of the program.]

Dear Moderator and Panelists:

Thank you for taking time to help us in the talkback for *The Thin Line*. What follows are some tips for getting the most out of this post-show opportunity and making it a successful, memorable, educational experience for the audience.

The goal of a post-show discussion is to get your community engaged and allow them to ask questions of the panelists. The Site Coordinator should inform you about the context of this program, what else has been done on the topic, and what is the future plan? Is there a perceived problem in the community?

It has been Add Verb's contractual policy that a panelist does *not* present as or reveal they are in recovery from an eating disorder. This stipulation is a protective measure for those in the audience who may be having difficulty, and to avoid unintentionally glamorizing the issues, or provide an opportunity for someone to think.

- *The Thin Line* is an intense play. Expect that it will take audiences a few minutes to transition and warm to a discussion.
- Keep your introduction brief. Modeling your own personal response to the performance will help break the ice with the audience. Credentials and relevant information can be shared along the way in the context of answering a question or in a playbill.
- When speaking, always use available microphones: most people think they don't need a microphone, but most do. Audibility is the consistently the biggest complaint and yet it is easily avoidable.

- If the Moderator hasn't done so, repeat or rephrase the question to be certain you heard the question properly and to make sure the whole audience has heard the question.
- Avoid asking yes/no questions of the audience as that does not generate discussion, and do not ask the audience to identify if they know someone with an eating disorder or someone who cuts himself or herself.
- Asking the audience an honest question, or one with different possible answers, can be an engaging strategy that will also serve to point out where they are in need of additional information.
- Don't be afraid of "wait time" when asking the audience a question. If you've asked a good question it may take them a few moments to respond.
- Try to provide as many different people as possible the opportunity to contribute to the discussion. Be aware of gender balance in participation, both on the panel and in the audience.
- While it may feel rude to interrupt if someone is dominating the conversation, the moderator may need to manage the time and pace of the discussion. Please stay succinct and on- topic, and evaluate whether another panelist has already said enough on a topic.
- Keep answers jargon-free in an age-appropriate language without being condescending.
- Avoid responding to overly personal questions from audience members, ask them to see you afterwards when you can better address their concern.
- "I don't know" is a legitimate answer.

Especially as there are so few opportunities for public discourse on eating disorders, you may feel pressured to share as much as you can about what you know. Instead, consider what to say that will invite people to have a longer conversation with you later.

THE THIN LINE PLOT SUMMARY
(Site Coordinator: please provide moderator and panelists with copies of this information.)

The Thin Line is a 30-minute one-woman play. It features four characters: a girl who is struggling with an eating disorder, her internal negative voice, her mother, and a friend. Great care has been taken with the script to give accurate information in a way that does not blame and does not offer how-to's, but instead illustrates how serious and pervasive eating disorders are. This program promotes early intervention, especially by the family and friends who are closest to people who are ill. What follows is a description of the story and action in *The Thin Line*. The actor switches characters simply and quickly from one character to the next with physicality, a costume item, or a small prop.

- Cindy is struggling with what to do as she recognizes unhealthy behaviors in her friend Ellen, and believes her to be in increasing danger.
- Ellen, a perceptive young woman and a driven athlete and artist, is aware of her eating disorder, is embarrassed by outsider judgments and assumptions, and is at the mercy of the negative voice inside her head.
- The Voice demonstrates her control over Ellen and Ellen's mind and behavior, explaining to the audience how myths and misconceptions about eating disorders make her "job" easier.
- Ellen progressively becomes more ill, recounting when she first began dieting and being conscious of her body and how social and family pressures and perceptions affect her.
- Ellen's Mother confesses how difficult and strange life and her daughter have become. She shares last night's events and the discovery that Ellen is also cutting herself. The Mother struggles with her own guilt, and fear of judgment on her family's situation.
- The Voice, in jeopardy now that Ellen is getting help, becomes even more vile in her treatment of Ellen, taking a

moment to talk to the audience about how language, socialization, and name calling can be devastating.
- Ellen's shame, anger, and frustration crest, and her health is in great jeaprody.
- Ellen's illness continues to impact Ellen and the whole family. Ellen's Mother shares more information on how, in spite of best efforts with medical care.
- Cindy has gotten professional help for herself thanks to the advice of her brother. He told her the story of his wrestling friend who is recovering from an eating disorder. The counselor helps Cindy set healthy boundaries with Ellen, and prepares her for an extremely difficult conversation.
- The Voice becomes more controlling and it is difficult for Ellen to differentiate between what is real and what is inside her head.
- Ellen is hospitalized. We get a window into Ellen's level of self-loathing, and the possiblility that she may not make it.
- The Voice flips through photos and reminisces over a wide range of people who have died from the illness.
- The Mother is now getting support to help her cope with her family's upheaval, and holds on to hope.
- Cindy is at last relieved of the burden of secrecy. With a strong support system in place, Cindy is prepared to be the friend she wants to be for Ellen: "Ellen may think she's alone, may tell me to leave her alone. But she's not alone. And neither am I. Thank you."

DISCUSSION FORMAT OPTIONS

Small groups? A large group discussion? Or a mix of large and small? There are advantages and drawbacks to both whole group and small group discussion formats. Add Verb has worked with a variety of audience types and encourages you design a post-performance experience that will work best for your community.

- Some follow *The Thin Line* with a single whole-group and panel discussion.
- Some do a whole-group and panel discussion with small group follow-ups (e.g., with advisors or homerooms).
- Some have had success supplementing the whole-group discussion with an invitation to audience members who wish to talk in greater depth about the issues to go to designated rooms where the conversation can continue with the panel members right afterwards (and, in schools, sending the rest of the audience back to classes). This can help honor the time limitations and still provide extra support for those who need it.

People often ask what is the biggest size audience that works. It depends on both the venue itself, and on what resources you have to run a good post show process immediately after the show.

SMALL GROUP DISCUSSION

Please provide small group facilitators some training to be sure they are comfortable and knowledgeable. Share **The Thin Line Plot Summary,** name what issues are prevalent in the school at the time, and be aware of any particulars about the community culture. Consider modeling a discusson, and role-playing how to handle different challenges. Facilitators should be asked to note their own self-awareness on fat-bias, weight, and mental illness, as well as issues around sexism and racism. Provide adults with a reminder about any mandated reporting regulations.

LARGE GROUP PANEL DISCUSSION

One of the biggest challenges of a large group discussion is balancing panel members' responses while encouraging audience participation. It can be easy for the panelists take over the conversation, but finding ways to get audience members involved enriches the program greatly. Some methods include:

- Provide note cards in the playbill programs or pass out note cards after the performance for audience members to write questions on. Runners can collect cards during the conversation, and an appointed person can organize, consolidate, and vet questions before handing to the Moderator.
- Provide one or two wireless microphones and roving helpers.
- Provide a microphone stand in the aisle and instruct people line up for questions.
- Position a spotter at the front to help find raised hands.
- When calling on an audience member, it can speed things along by identifying who will be called upon next.
- It is not a bad idea to plant a believable first question to break the ice.

It undermines all the work you've done when panelist can't be heard or when they don't let the audience hear the question asked. This is disrespectful and irritates audiences, who may be emotionally charged.

SAMPLE DISCUSSION APPROACH

1. Start with what the audience has just experienced. This will give a sense of where they are emotionally, and will begin to engage participation. For example:
- *What surprised you in this play? Why?*
- *Was this realistic? How so?*
- *What do you know now that you didn't know before?*

2. Move into what they already know. This will make it less lecture-like for them, and wil help you gauge what they already know. For example:
- *What are the different types of eating disorders?*
- *What are symptoms, medical complications and conditions that develop? How do people hide their condition?*
- *What does it mean to be healthy?*

Audiences are drawn in to the seriousness of the issue when they hear about some of the physical difficulties experienced with advanced eating disorders such as the erosion of the esophagus lining, tooth decay, the loss of a menstrual cycle, damage to vital organs, etc.

3. Questions to set EDs in a larger context could include:
- *If it's not about eating, what is it about?*
  Control, relationships, and stress, are among many other factors. (Caution: Connecting it to sexual abuse, while often true, may not be responsible in some settings.)
- *What connections can be made between eating disorders and other mental illness and self- destructive behaviors?*
  Addiction is something many people are culturally, if not personally familiar with, and recognize it to be a mental illness; some people with eating disorders try to hurt themselves with alcohol or drugs, some people cut themselves, others suffer from low-self esteem or depression. (Caution: there is frequently co-morbidity, but that is not always the case. For example, not everyone who cuts has an eating disorder; not everyone with an eating disorder cuts.)
- *What is the difference between disordered eating and an eating disorder?*

Not everyone who has a drink is an alcoholic, not everyone who diets has an eating disorder. Just as drugs and alcohol affect your brain and body's development and can lead to addiction, disordered eating hurts your brain and body, and can lead to an eating disorder.
- *How do you feel when people comment on the way you look? How could comments on looks be hurtful, either intentionally or unintentionally?*
- *Why is it important for people of all genders to know about eating disorders?*
- *Why are more and more male-identified people being diagnosed with eating disorders than ever before?*

Male-identified people have more pressure to be macho and buff than ever before and steroid use continues to be on the rise. Coaches and doctors are starting to become aware and so perhaps more are diagnosed. Certain sports are more prone to eating disorders: wrestling, swimming, gymnastics, and others.

4. **Plant seeds for futher action:**
   - *What if my friend has gotten help but it's still a problem?*
   The process of recovery is a just that--a process, and it is different for every person. The best thing you can do is get help for yourself and your own feelings to the situation, which can help you choose how to support your friend.
   - *What will you take away from the play and our discussion today?*

5. **Closing the discussion:**
   - It is vital that every audience member understand that support is available to them and that even though the program today has concluded, ther are people available for support.
   - Direct people to the play's program or other specific places to go for more information in the future.

IN THE DAYS AFTER THE THIN LINE

Thank you. You have provided your community with an opportunity and the tools to carry the conversation forward. An increased awareness about language and the dangers of eating disorders may help individuals to seek help. It may help those who have struggled with secrecy and shame find safe friends and adults to speak to. And, it may help send up an early alarm for those in danger.

You can be sure that someone desperately needed this play to happen. Time spent on this issue sends a message to those who have been silent that the community is willing to acknowledge their need.

Thank you for making a difference.

THE THIN LINE IN CULTURAL TRANSLATION: AUSTRALIA

The work done of creating a cultural translation for *The Thin Line* was preceeded by work done on another play. The collaboration with Ann Taket at Melbourne's Deakin University (Victoria, Australia) came about when she and I met in San Francisco at the American Public Health Conference in 2012. I was presenting initial findings on a longitudinal study regarding *You the Man*, a play on dating and sexual violence and bystander intervention, which was written by myself and touring as an Add Verb Production. *You the Man* is similarly constructed to *The Thin Line*, also with an accompanying education program.

Prof. Taket was interested in the completeness and brevity of these programs as public health interventions and community action tools. She found funding for cultural translations of both productions, and hosted me to assist with an Australian script of *You the Man* along with and a statewide tour to social service and education organizations that would potentially be interested in a program that furthered their own mission in addressing gender based violence.

It was exciting and gratifying to have the work find new life in another country and a new context. Our process was documented for an article co-written by the translation team and entitled The development and cultural translation of a brief theatre-based programme for the promotion of bystander engagement and violence prevention (*Journal of Applied Arts*, December 2014). Subsequently, Prof. Taket and her team adapted Add Verb's materials for touring and community engagement to create similar documents that would reflect resources local to Victoria.

Unlike my close involvement with the cultural translation of *You the Man*, my work on *The Thin Line* primarily meant approving any changes. While there are obvious places that the creative team of producers, writers, director and actors "Aussified" the script, the language is still remarkably similar to the US version.

The biggest changes in the Australian version are in moving one of the Voice's monologues to the front—with an update to include a tablet rather than an old-fashioned photo album—and in cutting lines for Jess (AU)/Cindy (US). I went back and forth on this requested to move the monologue as opening and closing the play with Jess/Cindy was intended to underscore the challenges of being a supportive friend to someone who is mentally ill. The writing team opted to change of the character's name to Jess was made because Cindy is not a common name in Australia, and the change met the goal of keeping the character of the friend as universal as possible.

The requests for changes that I did not agree to were really only regarding suggestions that I felt undercut a teaching point or were too coded, or too specific to a contemporary point of reference—and therefore immediately dated or would exclude those not in the know. While those suggestions certainly made the play sound "Australian" and very up-to-the-minute, I felt he priority was to keep the play as flexible as possible for audiences regardless their age—12, 22, or 42—and asked that some lines be restored or made more generic.

But all in all, *The Thin Line* required relatively easy and cosmetic adjustments in order to make it resonate with Australian youth and adult audiences. The requirements for *You the Man* were much more culturally nuanced and complex.

CP

THE THIN LINE
by Cathy Plourde
Australian script adapted by Ann Taket, Virginia Murray, Genevieve Pepin, and Patrick Van Der Werf. Directed by Suzanne Chaundy and produced by Prof. Ann Taket (Deakin University, Melbourne, Victoria)

Copyright © CATHY PLOURDE. 2000, 2002, 2009, 2015, 2016.

DO NOT DUPLICATE OR DISTRIBUTE OR PERFORM WITHOUT PERMISSION FROM PLAYWRIGHT
Cathy Plourde holds exclusive right to production. For licensing information or other queries, including permission to quote, contact addverblicensing@gmail.com

THE THIN LINE: AUSTRALIA

1. THE VOICE

Arrives with tablet, shoulder bag, and sunglasses ready for work.

(To audience) Hello, hello. Just checking my account.

Scrolling tablet

This woman here… a $200 a day food habit. Went shopping on the way home from work, buying exactly the same things she bought the day before, didn't wait to get home to start eating, didn't stop until she ate everything she just bought, threw it up, and went to bed. Next day, did the same thing all over. Kidney failure.

Types post

Eat it but don't keep it. Way to go. Ha Ha.

(To audience) Some of my best work.

Now this one. No one has any idea she has an eating order.

Types post

You deserve an Oscar.

(To audience) And look this guy here – here, a size 64 waist pants, here, size 32. Same person. Heart failure.

This girl, bone density of an eighty year old.

Types post

Happy birthday, sweet sixteen.

Ah, and here's my latest...

Types post

Elly, I can see that belly.

(To audience) Ohh, and here's her poor concerned friend.

2. JESS

This lady just asked me how I was going. I said "oh-fine!" I should have said: *I'm not bad – could be worse – I could have an eating disorder like my friend Ellen.* I'd like to see what would have happened if I had told her how I really am: *Well, my best friend's been on a series of crazy diets, has been throwing up for I don't know how long, has made me promise not to tell, and basically is scaring the hell out of me. Thanks for asking, and how are you?* I'm sure she was just being polite – but how many times do people ask 'how are you?' and you say 'fine!' because you're expected to say 'fine' and move on. Maybe it's a game and if I pretend it's fine it will be fine.

I'm over pretending and it's not a game. My best friend Ellen is dying a slow death. I'm not being dramatic. This is real. What do I do now? Do I risk our friendship and tell? If I tell and no one does anything will I lose my friend for good? Doesn't anybody else see she's got a problem? Why doesn't her netball coach see it? What about her parents? And if they do see what's happening and can't do anything, what makes me think I could help her? If I don't say anything it's like I'm agreeing with her. But I don't agree. And the longer I don't say anything, the worse she gets, disappearing before our eyes. I need to know what to do.

3. ELLEN

(ELLEN is seated with her art supplies and several pieces of art-board--her work. She is wearing an oversized shirt. She shading in an area of a picture. She's tired of the questions. And she knows people are waiting.)

"Ellen, what's the matter with you?" What's my problem? I could ask what's yours. Why do I have to have a problem before anybody cares I exist? And then I still don't exist because they don't see me, they see someone with an eating disorder. It didn't happen instantly, like I crossed over a line or something. So what did happen? How did I get right here, right now? Is it the media's fault? *News flash: Girl Killed By* Famous *and* Vogue; Health and Fitness *Suspected Accomplice.* If looking at models and actors was all it took, wouldn't everyone have an eating disorder? Was I abused? Do you think I'd tell you? I know it happens. Am I trying to get attention? Well aren't we all? So, have I got horrible parents? Or am I just crazy? Yeah, well, this world is crazy. You've gotta walk a thin line to get by... Be smart, but not too smart. Be pretty, but not too pretty or everybody thinks you're a snob, or everybody thinks you don't have a brain. The rules change everyday and everything

stays the same. Everybody just assumes they know everything about you when you aren't even sure you know yourself. After a while, that voice inside your head is the only one that makes any sense...

4. THE VOICE

(Actor leaves ELLEN'S oversized shirt on the chair, and crosses upstage to the stool. She puts on her sunglasses to become the VOICE. Loud and boisterous, slick and slimy, sugary sweet and sincerely insincere, and always charming, THE VOICE has ELLEN under her control.)

Goooooood morning! It's rise and shine, and — *(She dumps out the cup of brushes and markers.)* — hold it right there, Ellen, because I'm your first waking thought! Now, what is it you are NOT going to eat today, and how will you burn off all the calories you're charged with for even thinking about food? Little Miss Perfect, Miss Goody-Two-Shoes... you're about as perfect as dirt — how can you even be seen in public??

(To Audience.) Oh — who am I? Why, I'm Ms Negativity, Ellen's personal trainer, and I'm in charge around here now.

(To Ellen, glasses are back on.) Now where were we...let's see...ah, the gut, yes, your flabby, ugly, fat belly. Disgusting. Whenever you stand up in class or meet someone new or walk down the street, ask yourself what do they think of you and YOUR BIG FAT STOMACH, Ellie-Belly, got that?

(She removes her glasses coming down to address the audience directly.)

Wait, the rest of you out there are wondering what right do I have, where do I get my nerve, telling this girl to hate her body? What you don't understand is that her world is spinning out of control and she just happens to believe that she can control this one part of her life, that she can change her body. She's not alone—there's a world out there just dying to be thin, stuck in a web of myths and misconceptions. Myth number one is that an eating disorder is a 'rich white girl syndrome'. Actually, more and more boys are falling prey, and I couldn't care less how much money you and your family's got or what color your skin is. Second is the beauty myth. The 24/7 media feeds the obsession with celebrities and dictates standards of beauty—never mind that it took a team of eight and photo-shopped body parts to get the perfect photo of that cover girl. Third, we have health professionals who make the girl out to be a nutter, while really, what's happening is only a symptom of what's wrong—wrong with the world, wrong with her, wrong with you. And finally, the biggest misconception of all is that the problem is ELLEN. And since no one is willing to talk about it...well, that just makes it all the easier. And, I'm turning up the volume...

(She reloads her sunglasses, and steps between ELLEN's chair and the table. Back to business.)

Yes, Ellen. It's me in continuous play in your head, building on your worst nightmares, your secret fears. The medical term "anorexia" *(She has written the word out on the drawing pad, and rips it out before showing it to the audience and then tossing it aside.)* means 'absence of hunger or appetite' but you and I alone know that that's not true. You have a huge appetite, you're extremely hungry, but you're willing to deny yourself your existence. They say "bulimia" *(Again, writes, rips it out, shares it, but crumples the sheet into a wad.)* is an oxen hunger, an uncontrolled consumption... and that's not true either because you and me kid, we can control it, and if need be we can make sure that what goes in WILL come out. *(Tosses paper, peeks out over sunglasses)* And you people out there are going to sit and watch her swallow herself whole.

5. ELLEN

(Leaving sunglasses on DR corner of the table, she steps out, and puts on the oversized shirt. She sees the mess on the floor, and sees the audience see that mess.

During the following speech everything gets put away – papers smoothed and clipped in the drawing pad, pens and marker put into the pencil box, secured with an elastic. One piece of artwork gets left out for later.)

Well the first time I went on a diet and really started exercising was when I was ten. Maybe nine. It was the summer I spent with my friend Jess's family down the Coast. Jess and I would exercise with her older sister every morning and then spend the day at the beach. We lived in our bathers the whole time. Well, Jess lived in her bathers; *I* lived in my bathers and an over-sized T-shirt. That's when things started to change. You know, with my body. Suddenly, everything's about make-up and clothes and friends and who's got a boyfriend, and whether or not you've had sex yet.

When I was little, my father's annoying nickname for me was Ellie-Belly...well, I got home after that holiday and my father said 'Ellie! No more belly! Now what do I call you?' *How about using my name, Dad?* But he was right. My belly was gone. And that felt good.

You know, everyone does it — even the girls who aren't really on diets pretend to be because everyone else is doing it...and if my friend is thinner than me and she's on a diet, well, maybe that means I'm fat, maybe that means I should be on a diet, too. It's like being in a club...or like getting the same kind of clothes as everyone else...it's what you have to do. It's a game, a contest to see who's the best expert on rice cakes, fat-grams, laxatives, how to fool your parents into thinking you've eaten, and how many times to run up and down the stairs to burn off one piece of chocolate. *(She's taken off the over-shirt for this last line, and leaves it crumpled on the table.)*

6. JESS

Ellen and I would always exercise together, but then, when it was clear that she had a problem, it made me not want to go with her anymore. I did keep going with her because I felt as though I should keep an eye on her, you know, in case something happened. I felt responsible and I felt like I should help her. But continuing to go to the gym with her certainly wasn't helping. I was making *myself* sick – sick with worry. And I have my own problems to deal with. *I* don't starve myself and then eat the fridge clean to solve *my* problems. *(She feels bad for saying this.)* I really thought about giving up. *(To ELLEN)* ...Fine, if you want to kill yourself trying to be thin, well fine, if that's what makes you happy. *(To audience)* Except Ellen is not happy. And neither am I.

7. THE MOTHER

(Crossing left to MUM'schair, she puts on her reading glasses. After regarding her daughter's "room", MUM approaches the table, neatening the crumpled shirt and looking at the artwork during the following.)

She was the perfect baby. No trouble, ever. She was always happy. Now she only looks happy when she's asleep or doing her art. She's such a perfectionist... *(the irony of her own perfectionism isn't lost on her.)* I thought at first that what Ellen was going through was just a time where she was pulling away, growing up, trying to be her own person...I thought the best thing to do was just leave her alone, to back off. I had no idea. It's hard to believe that the Ellen who created this *(indicating the art)*, is the same Ellen who transforms into a monster, crying, screaming, swearing, throwing, punching, scratching. Like a caged animal. Like we are the enemy. We had a fight last night, and finally, we just held her. Her father and I stood there, with her in between us, and we held her until we could feel the rage wash out of her body, leaving her limp, hardly conscious. We put her to bed, like we did when she was a baby, and we got her into her pyjamas. It's awful to see how little there is to her body...and worse – how could it be worse?

Her arms and her stomach were covered with thin lines. Some hardly perceptible, others quite fresh with scabs. It took me a few moments before I realized what this was. Ellen has been cutting herself. More torture. More pain.

> *(She's become upset but upset but confronts the audience.)*

You look at me and you ask yourself could it be 'the mother's fault'? Or 'did her father push her too hard'? Did we put her on a diet? Did we teach her that in order to be worth anything, what matters are her looks, her body, instead of her mind and her love? *I don't know.* Don't you think if there was something simple to be done to fix it all, her father and I would have tried it already? If you content yourself with blaming us then none of us have to stop and figure out how we can fix this.

7. THE VOICE

> *(Spins and leaves MUM's glasses DL on the table, swapping them for the sunglasses.)*

(To the audience:) Fix it? Fix it, like a broken shoe or television? Ha! Give me time, and I'll take the parents out, too. *(Placing herself back in ELLEN's space.)* They say they love you. But Ellen, your parents are going to look at you one day real soon, at you, their precious daughter, and they'll let you know that they hate you. You'll see it in your father's eyes and you'll hear it in your mum's voice, and then, yes, next time when I tell you something you'll listen.

> *(Crossing DSC, removing glasses. She's speaking to the audience, cold and clinical.)*

You're fed the thin line early on. Somehow those messages everybody gets growing up — be nice, be good, be responsible, avoid conflict, put others before yourself, don't hurt other people's feelings even if it means ignoring your own. Somehow those messages become monsters. Fat Cow. Hey, Fatty Boombah. Fatty-fatty-two-by-four/can't fit through the kitchen door. Innocent name-calling? Sticks and stones can break my bones, but names...names will scar you for life. Oh, excuse me — I can't leave her alone for a moment. *(She has noticed that ELLEN needs to be put back into line. The VOICE invades ELLEN's chair, puts on the shirt, and has taken over.)* What did your neighbor just say to you? *Ellen, you look healthy today!?* You know what that means, what *healthy* means — that means you look fat, fat like her, that's what she's trying to do to you, make you fat like her. Drop and give me twenty. Now, Ellie!

> *(Crosses DS of the table, does crunches, fast and furious. We can hear her exertion. She struggles to her feet, now as ELLEN, leaving the sunglasses on the desk, defensively repositioning behind the table.)*

9. ELLEN

I know how hideous I look. This is not fun for me. People think it's a big joke. They talk behind my back. Or they talk to me like I'm a baby who can't understand anything. Or like I'm going to fall apart any second. It'd be nice to not be treated like I was a walking contagious disease by people who used to be my friends. There used to be more to know about me than how many ounces I've gained or lost today, but that's all my mother and father and doctors care about. It's not that I don't want to grow up, it just that things get harder and harder to control, and you get more and more responsibility at the same time. I'm dying to be heard, to find someone who understands. I'm trying. I've got all the responsibility I can handle now. I don't want any more.

> *(She sweeps everything off the table in fury and frustration.)*

They tell me I'm at a crossroads. My blood pressure can't go any lower or I will die. They ask me why I don't want to live. Of course I want to live. Why don't they ask me questions I can answer? I am so ashamed. *(She leaves the shirt on the table.)*

10. THE MOTHER

> *(MUM puts on her glasses.)*

I'm almost ashamed to admit it, but we were scared. It was a relief when Ellen started eating again. We pulled through, as a family, and we thought the worst was over. A commitment to what was important — it was hard sometimes but also nice. Healthy foods, mealtimes together. Help from therapists, dieticians, doctors — wonderful professionals who told us so much we needed to know. But it was the ants that told us the truth. Ants marching in and out of the wardrobe in the spare room. The pest exterminator asked us why we stored so much snack food in that wardrobe, and told us we might want to use Ziplock bags or Tupperware instead of shoe boxes, for food, and that would prevent ants from being attracted to our spare room. Do you understand? That's how we found out about Ellen's binging, hording food, and binging. We had thought she was better. Now, the drains haven't been working right, and this week we got home to find half the house flooded, a pipe burst. The plumbers suggested that we don't put food down the drain. The way they said it, they knew. They were just being polite, apparently they had seen this before. They didn't want to say to me or my husband that the reason the pipes have burst is because your daughter has thrown up so much food that the pipes couldn't handle it. We had thought she was getting better. We thought we were handling it. We thought things were working out.

11. JESS

(The actor leaves the reading glasses behind, and sits in the down right chair. She is very agitated, and can't sit for long.)

I talked to a couple friends, but they weren't exactly helpful. Everybody seems to know someone who's got a problem and no one knows what to do. The best advice I got was from my brother Brett, of all people, and he said his friend Matt got all freaky about food because he had to keep his weight down for footy. It got so bad he passed out in the sauna trying to lose weight before anyone figured out there was a problem, and he wound up in the hospital for weeks. Matt's well enough now to come to classes, but he's not going to go back to footy anytime soon. Something about his heart and electrolytes. It's that serious. My brother said if I was really that worried about Ellen

I should talk to the counselor who's working with Matt. And based on what's happened I'm glad I did.

No matter how much I want to help her to get better, I can't get better for her. She has to do it. And I have to be honest with her. I have to be honest with her until she can learn to be honest with herself. So, I finally talked to Ellen.

(To ELLEN) I can't go to the gym with you anymore, because I'm scared, because I feel like I'm helping you abuse yourself. Get some help, I told her, and I'll go with you if you want or just call a help line... She was pissed off. No, I mean really pissed off. And she said things that no friend would ever say. Then she informed me that she didn't need help because she was in control.

Ellen was admitted to the hospital a few days ago, and they don't know how long she'll have to be there. I'm trying not to think about it, trying not to think that maybe if I had said something sooner...maybe if I had tried to...if I could have...No. I can't think like that. It wasn't my fault. For the first time in months, I was telling her the truth.

12. VOICE

(Puts on glasses, DS of table.)

To be honest, I couldn't tell you why I can make some people develop an eating disorder, and yet leave others unaffected. Everyone's different. I try to get them young, but any age is fine with me: fifty, fifteen, five... By the time they realize they're *not* in control... well...

13. ELLEN

(Leaves sunglasses on DS edged table, she drapes her overshirt over her shoulders, clutching as if cold. Then, as she turns to face center, it is clear how ill Ellen is.)

At first... I felt powerful, strong...and now...I can hardly... It's not about eating. But it's the one thing I can control. My life is out of control, and no one will leave me alone. I'm sick of this. And so afraid. I know I am walking a thin line. I'm so disgusting. You don't know. I don't think I can do this.

(She turns her back to the audience, slowly removes the shirt and drops it on the floor.)

14. THE MOTHER

(With reading glasses, she turns to take in the audience and then sees she must deal with ELLEN's shirt that's on the floor.)

I don't know what will happen. That's the hardest part. Some days are better than others. I hated the eating disorder. It sounds selfish, but I resented it interfering with how I want to live my life. It's a parasite bent on destroying its host. It crept into my daughter's mind, into our house and into our lives, and I wanted it to go—*leave us alone, give us back our family.* But that's not how it works. The eating disorder isn't Ellen, but is a part of Ellen, and it's hard, but it needs just as much love as the rest of her. I need to love all of Ellen.

(She leaves the glasses and shirt on the table and crosses to the back of JESS's chair, DR.)

15. JESS

They finally let me see her. I said, *Ellen, we're friends. No matter what you say or do, it will not change that we are friends.* When I told her that, for that moment, I had her, like I had gotten through just a little bit. She seems intent on testing me, and twisting what I say, just to see if I mean it, to see what is real. But at least now I don't feel like I am carrying her secret. There are people who know what's going on, and together we hope...we hope we can make it. Ellen may think she's alone, may tell me to leave her alone, but she's not alone. And neither am I. Thank you.

Add Verb Productions 89

90 The Thin Line

Add Verb Productions 91

www.ingramcontent.com/pod-product-compliance
Lightning Source LLC
Chambersburg PA
CBHW060211050426
42446CB00013B/3049